Sushi

Sushi

A Pocket Guide

by Minori Fukuda & Kit Shan Li

CHRONICLE BOOKS
SAN FRANCISCO

Library of Congress Cataloging-in-Publication Data available.

ISBN 0-8118-4504-4

Manufactured in China

Designed by Work Eat Studio
Photographed by Raeanne Giovanni-Inoue
Food prepared by Masayuki Nakano

Distributed in Canada by Raincoast Books
9050 Shaughnessy Street
Vancouver, British Columbia V6P 6E5

10 9 8 7 6 5 4 3 2 1

Chronicle Books LLC
85 Second Street
San Francisco, California 94105

www.chroniclebooks.com

ATTENTION PLEASE !!

Sushi often uses raw ingredients; don't be surprised by uncooked elements, including fish. Dishes by the same name as those in this book may differ from restaurant to restaurant. If you are a vegetarian or have food allergies, please consult the servers or the restaurant manager before you order. Relax and enjoy your sushi. Thank you!

MENU

INTRODUCTION
8

Chapter 1
NIGIRI
20

Chapter 2
MAKI
52

Chapter 3
SPECIAL DISHES AND UNUSUAL SUSHI
70

ACKNOWLEDGMENTS
78

BIOGRAPHIES
79

INTRODUCTION

About This Book

Sushi is a pocket-size reference book based on the global dining experiences of its sushi-loving authors. Together and separately, we have crossed chopsticks in sushi restaurants from New York to Tokyo. The purpose of this book is to help anyone unfamiliar with sushi to decide which dishes might appeal to them. Whether you are more experienced or completely uninitiated with sushi, this book can act as your host to this delicious and artistic Japanese cuisine. Enjoy sushi with friends!

How to Use This Book

Following you'll find a brief history of sushi, general information on how to order it and how to eat it, and a glossary explaining the primary elements. Thereafter, the book is arranged in three chapters based on categories of sushi: Chapters 1 and 2 cover the two basic types, *nigiri* and *maki*, and Chapter 3 is dedicated to unusual sushi toppings and some special dishes. Each entry is accompanied by a photograph; its name in Japanese characters; the Japanese name in the Western alphabet, broken into syllables to assist pronunciation; the English translation of the name; and a brief description. In addition, each type of sushi is coded with icons to indicate at a glance whether that particular kind of sushi is raw or cooked and if it is vegetarian, as follows:

Cooked   Vegetarian

The History of Sushi

The exact origins of sushi are uncertain. One beginning of sushi making seems to lie in the Japanese introduction to a Southeast Asian method of preserving raw fish by packing it between layers of rice. Then, reportedly in the eighteenth century, a man named Hanaya Yohei opened an eatery in the Ryogoku district of Tokyo, where he served raw seafood on small fingers of vinegared rice, making him possibly the first to sell sushi similar to the nigiri-zushi of today.

Around the turn of the nineteenth century, during the Edo period, nigiri as we know it was invented in the Tokyo bay area, where fresh fish and seaweed were readily available. With the appeal of easy eating made possible by the presentation of a choice bit of seafood on a pad of rice, sushi began its reign of popularity.

In time, sushi spread to other parts of Japan, partly as a result of the great earthquake of 1923 in Tokyo. The devastation of that event was so great that most businesses had to close and huge numbers of people were forced to flee Tokyo and return to their hometowns—among them, many of the city's sushi chefs.

Today, there is a huge variety of sushi available in Japan and elsewhere, and the mingling of international tastes has created a give and take within the indigenous cuisine. The California roll, for example, originated in the United States, but is now available in Japan. The story of sushi will continue to evolve, because the popularity of sushi around the globe will continue to expand with the possibilities of toppings and forms.

Types of Sushi

There are two primary categories of sushi found at most sushi restaurants outside of Japan. The individual pieces of sushi shaped by hand with bites of topping are called *nigiri-zushi*, also known as *edomae-zushi*. Nigiri originated in the Tokyo area. The second category of common sushi comprises rolls called *nori-maki* and the handrolls called *temaki*. The former are rolls of rice stuffed with fish, vegetables, or a combination that have been wrapped in nori (seaweed), rolled into cylinders in a small bamboo mat, called *makisu*, and sliced into bite-size portions. The latter are larger cones of nori filled with the ingredients and eaten with the hands rather than with chopsticks.

Nigiri-zushi   Nori-maki   Temaki

Another type of sushi that you might find is *hako-zushi*, a bed of rice layered with fish and/or vegetables and pressed in a box into wide, flat squares. Hako-zushi is rarely found in restaurants outside Japan.

Note that *sashimi* refers to thinly sliced portions of raw fish served plain without rice. Typically the fish served as sashimi are also offered as nigiri (see Chapter 1).

Sushi Restaurants

In the typical sushi restaurant, you can choose a seat either
at the bar in front of the sushi chefs or at a table. If you sit
at the bar, you have the advantage of glimpsing the action of
the cuisine's artistry, and possibly a recommendation directly
from the chefs, or simply friendly conversation. Use this book
and don't be afraid to ask questions; they are generally happy
to assist you with their expertise.

Kaiten-zushi restaurants are self-service sushi restaurants.
These are generally less expensive and less formal than regular
sushi restaurants. Usually the seating is around a counter,
where you will find plates of sushi circulating on a conveyor
belt. Each plate usually has a pair of sushi on it. You serve
yourself by picking up your choices and then stacking your
empty plates beside you. Each plate is coded by size or color
to figure the price at the end of your meal.

Kaiten-zushi

How to Order Sushi

Use all available resources, including friends, restaurant staff, and this book, to assist you in ordering sushi. Learn your favorites, and explore new toppings, as there are often unexpected delights with sushi!

Omakase (Chef's Choice of the Day)
This is the way to order when you want to eat fresh sushi selected by the chef. Simply set a budget; tell the chef or waitperson perhaps "5,000 yen no Omakase de," or about $50 in U.S. currency. This is a fine approach if you don't know what to order or if you're interested in trying anything your hosts recommend.

5,000 yen no Omakase de

How to Eat Sushi

Once the ordering is done, you may feel a bit uncertain as to how to tackle your sushi. Here are the basic techniques.

1 Pour out some soy sauce into the small sauce dish provided at your place setting.

2 Stir some wasabi (see page 19) into your pool of soy sauce, according to your heat tolerance. (Sushi chefs usually put a dab of wasabi underneath each sushi topping, so be careful not to use too much.)

3 Pick up the sushi piece with your fingers.
(You may also use chopsticks, but using one's
fingers is the traditional way.)

GOOD　　　　　　**BETTER**

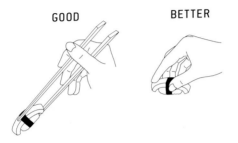

4 Dip the sushi, topping side down, in the soy sauce,
being careful not to break the rice apart.
That way, you won't soak up too much soy sauce.

ONE BITE ONLY, TWO IF YOU MUST

Glossary

Noren
The *noren* is a short curtain hanging over the entrance of many
Japanese stores, especially sushi restaurants, public baths, and
traditional Japanese food stores. They were originally used as
sunshades; today you see them used more as the "face" of each
store. The noren usually features the store logo or name. When
the noren is in place, it means the store is open for business;
when it is not, it means the store is closed.

Itamae
Sushi chefs are called *itamae* in Japanese, which means "in front
of the (cutting) board." Sushi chefs stand behind a counter in
view of customers while preparing the freshly made sushi.
They often wear white, with a cloth around their head, to
demonstrate cleanliness. They typically use a cutting board
made of light-colored wood to further emphasize the sanitary
ethos of sushi. Another imperative in sushi is the chef's skill.
Most sushi chefs are trained under masters while working at
sushi restaurants. It takes about ten years to become a fully
skillful and knowledgeable sushi chef.

Ohashi (Chopsticks)
Except for eating sushi, when using fingertips is the norm, chopsticks are the traditional Asian utensil for dining. Asian restaurants often provide disposable wooden chopsticks for other dishes or for those who prefer them for picking up their sushi. To avoid slivers, unwrap wooden chopsticks and polish them with each other before using.

Agari (Green Tea)
Agari, or green tea (also called *ocha*), is the traditional drink with sushi. The tea acts as a palate cleanser.

Miso Shiru (Miso Soup)
Miso soup is the typical and well-loved starter for a Japanese meal. The famously comforting broth usually contains tofu, scallion, seaweed, and miso (a distinctive rich, salty paste made with fermented soybeans). In Japan, miso soup is not eaten with a spoon but is sipped from the bowl by holding it with both hands.

Geta (Sushi Plate)
Sushi is traditionally served on a *geta*,
a wooden plate with small wooden feet.
You may also see other decorative plates,
such as hand-painted ceramics.

Neta (Topping)
Neta, the topping placed over the rice,
is the main ingredient of sushi. It must
be sized for perfect balance with the rice
beneath it.

Shari (Vinegared Rice)
A small portion of a special preparation of
vinegared rice is placed underneath the neta
for nigiri or around it for maki. The right
rice for sushi is essential; it must be the
perfect amount, texture, and temperature.

Nori (Seaweed)
Nori is dried seaweed in sheet form. It is
used to wrap sushi rolls, and is also used
as a garnish.

Murasaki (Soy Sauce)
Also called *shoyu*. Sometimes you have a choice of soy sauces; bottles with a red cap are typically regular, and those with green caps are of lower sodium. Sometimes restaurants offer fresh soy sauce, which is reddish and transparent rather than dark in color.

Wasabi (Asian Horseradish)
This spicy green condiment excites the palate and counters the stronger aromas of some sushi. Be aware that the chef usually adds a small amount of wasabi underneath the topping, so be careful not to put too much in the soy sauce you prepare for dipping. Wasabi is sometimes prepared by simply grating the fresh root but more often by adding a small amount of water to dried, powdered wasabi. You can also find wasabi paste sold in tubes at Asian markets.

Gari (Pickled Ginger)
This distinctly pink accompaniment to sushi is thinly sliced, pickled ginger root. Its function is to refresh your mouth between flavors.

CHAPTER 1

にぎり

Nigiri

For sushi fans, a mouthful of nigiri, made with a bite of impeccably fresh raw fish on top of vinegared rice, is the purest pleasure. For beginners, the notion of eating raw fish can be a little daunting. We recommend beginning with *hamachi* (yellowtail), *toro* (fatty tuna), or *sake* (salmon), which are tender and melt in your mouth; or start with cooked nigiri such as *ebi* (shrimp) or *unagi* (barbecued eel). Keep an open mind while exploring the indescribably delicate and tasty flavors of the sea at their freshest. Many restaurants also offer vegetarian nigiri such as cucumber or avocado.

Toro can be the most expensive topping among all the sushi choices. The meat closer to the bone is pink or red; the meat just underneath the skin is whiter.

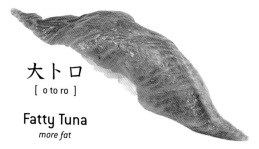

大トロ
[o to ro]

Fatty Tuna
more fat

O-toro is the fattest cut from the tuna's belly. The meat is pinkish and soft, and melts in your mouth.

中トロ
[chu to ro]

Medium Fatty Tuna
less fat

Chu-toro is soft and smooth like o-toro but less oily and a deeper shade of pink.

マグロ

[ma gu ro]

Tuna

deep red flesh; dense but very tender; a little oily

さけ
[sa ke]

Salmon

orange flesh; dense; rich tasting

Sake is sometimes pronounced "sha-ke."
The flavor has a wide appeal;
sake is very popular in the United States.

ひらめ
[hi ra me]

Flounder

tender, although a little tough to bite on at first;
clean taste; very subtle sweetness

Good for beginners who want to experience
raw fish with a mild flavor.

はまち
[ha ma chi]

Yellowtail

very dense but tender;
slightly sweet at first bite with a mild, sweet aftertaste

たい
[tai]

Sea Bream

firm and slightly pungent

Japanese eat tai for special occasions
such as New Year celebrations and weddings.

さわら
[sa wa ra]

Spanish Mackerel

usually prepared with the outside skin lightly seared
but the inside still raw; tender; mildly sweet

あじ
[a j i]

Horse Mackerel

pink meat with silvery skin; tender;
savory saltiness combined with a sweetness
that lasts long on the palate

Another popular white fish topping.

すずき
[su zu ki]

Sea Bass

pale peach flesh; quite firm, dense, and juicy;
subtly sweet with an extra note of fish in the aftertaste

さより

[sa yo ri]

Halfbeak

soft texture; mildly sweet with a plain flavor
Fish with silvery skin like this are usually vinegared.

こはだ
[ko ha da]

Shad

pungent; coarse texture; salty;
slightly sour because seasoned with vinegar

かつお

[ka tsu o]

Bonito

Katsuo is served with flavorful skin, usually eaten with grated ginger or garlic to counter the strong aroma.

とり貝
[to ri gai]

Cockle

Torigai is usually boiled briefly to eliminate the odor.
Check with your chef or server before ordering.

あおやぎ

[a o ya gi]

Trough-Shell Round Clam

medium-firm; bouncy texture; sweet and mild

Aoyagi is Kit's favorite clam.

みる貝
[mi ru gai]

Giant Clam

firm and chewy/crunchy; sweet

This is Kit's sister's favorite,
even though she doesn't eat any other raw fish.

ほたて
[ho ta te]

Scallop

tender; extremely mild flavor compared to most mollusks

The meat of this shellfish melts in your mouth,
with a consistency similar to gelatin.
Minori likes eating this as sashimi,
with soy sauce and wasabi.

あわび
[a wa bi]

Abalone

beach (sandy) aroma; chewy/crunchy; lightly juicy

This shellfish can be rather pricy, but it's delicious and worth the expense. It may be offered raw or cooked.

There are several varieties of shrimps and prawns.
They can be served raw or cooked.

車えび
[ku ru ma e bi]

Japanese Prawn

a mild nutty flavor, the meat is much tougher
and bigger than amaebi or botanebi

甘えび
[a ma e bi]

Sweet Shrimp

tender; chews to a pleasant, rich paste

This variety of shrimp is indeed sweeter than other shrimp,
with a luxurious and soft texture.

ぼたんえび

[bo tan e bi]

Jumbo Sweet Shrimp

A larger version of amaebi.

うなぎ
[u na gi]

Freshwater Eel

river eel; coarse texture; earthy aroma; slightly chewy skin;
has small edible bones with a pleasant crunch

Usually unagi is barbecued, with a sweet-savory sauce
brushed on before serving. Very popular and delicious choice
in general, though eel may seem strange to first-timers.

あなご
[a na go]

Conger Eel

sea eel; tender; oily; has a much softer meat than unagi

Anago may be served with a special sauce,
but we recommend eating it with a small amount of sauce
so that the distinctive taste isn't lost.

たこ

[ta ko]

Octopus

mild sweet; tough; very chewy

Because of the highly chewy consistency of octopus,
tako is always boiled before further preparation.

いか
[i ka]

Squid

very mild; chewy and gluey; slightly salty

かに
[ka ni]

Lump Crab Meat

very mild
Typically the crab used for kani is taraba-gani, or king crab.

うに
[u ni]

Sea Urchin

Uni is our favorite, although not everyone enjoys this
unusual experience. The extreme creaminess melts on the
sushi rice, indescribable but wonderful . . .
the ocean never tasted so sweet!
Kit enjoys it pure, without soy sauce.
Minori likes it with a touch of soy sauce and wasabi.

いくら
[i ku ra]

Salmon Roe

strong aroma; very salty; juicy

The bright orange pearls of salmon roe release a pop of
liquid flavor when the delicate skins break in your mouth,
making a great combination with the rice.

とびこ

[to bi ko]

Flying Fish Roe

sweet/salty; crunchy; slightly juicy

You can hear the crunch of the skins bursting
when you bite into the tiny, bright orange beads of tobiko,
a mild-flavored roe. Sometimes you see
masago (smelt roe), which is from shishamo fish.
The color is very similar to tobiko, but smaller in size.

数の子

[ka zu no ko]

Herring Roe

natural yellow color; slightly salty;
rubbery texture with a bit of bitterness

This topping is one of the traditional features
at Japanese New Year celebrations.

玉子

[ta ma go]

Egg

Tamago is a favorite among vegetarians, small children,
and fish lovers alike. It is a layered preparation that requires
a lot of skill to make. Because it is sweetened with sugar,
in Japan some people order tamago as a dessert; but this specialty
is also sometimes ordered first, to measure the chef's skill.

CHAPTER 2

巻き

Maki

Maki, or sushi rolls, combine fish and/or vegetables with sushi rice in a seaweed wrapper in the form of a roll. The rolls come in two primary forms: *nori-maki*, in which the nonrice ingredients form a core within a cylinder of pressed rice that is usually wrapped in seaweed and then cut into bite-size pieces; and *temaki*, larger, unpressed cones of several bites. Among maki you will find vegetarian options and smaller morsels of fish that may be more palatable to those new to sushi.

鉄火
[te kka]

Tuna

thin roll with a core of maguro (tuna)

ねぎとろ
[ne gi to ro]

Minced Fatty Tuna & Scallion

thin roll stuffed with minced toro (fatty tuna) and scallion

かっぱ

[ka ppa]

Cucumber

thin roll with a core of cucumber

Some people order this roll to test the quality
of the sushi rice; one can easily taste the rice
because the cucumber has a bland flavor.

おしんこ
[o shin ko]

Pickled Radish

thin roll with a core of oshinko

Oshinko has a somewhat odd,
pungent smell but a pleasant crunchy texture and sweet taste.

かんぴょう

[kam pyo]

Gourd

Kampyo is a dried gourd similar to squash,
it's prepared with soy sauce and sugar.

太巻
[fu to ma ki]

Futo Maki

Futo maki is originally from Osaka.
Ingredients for futo maki vary from restaurant to restaurant;
common ingredients are cucumber, egg, kampyo (dried gourd),
mitsuba ("three leaves"), and shiitake mushroom.
Vegetarians should note that some restaurants make futo maki
with fish or shrimp inside; ask your server.

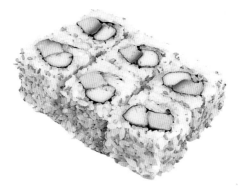

カリフォルニアロール
California Roll

crabmeat, cucumber, and avocado,
coated with either sesame seeds or tobiko (flying fish roe)

This sushi is not a traditional roll from Japan,
but it has become popular almost everywhere.

レインボーロール

Rainbow Roll

ebi (shrimp) and assorted raw fish wrapped around
a California roll

ボストンロール

Boston Roll

ebi (shrimp), lettuce, cucumber, avocado

スパイダーロール

Spicy Tuna Roll

Recipes for spicy tuna vary.
Most typically it is coarsely chopped tuna seasoned
with chili powder and mixed with a little mayonnaise.

フィラデルフィアロール

Philadelphia Roll

smoked salmon, cream cheese

Although this innovation is popular in the States, our chef
dislikes the mismatch of cream cheese and sushi rice.

えび天ぷらロール

Shrimp Tempura Roll

ebi tempura (battered and deep fried shrimp),
cucumber, avocado

ドラゴンロール

Dragon Roll

unagi (barbecued eel), avocado, cucumber,
tobiko (flying fish roe)

This popular roll combines
cooked (unagi) and raw (tobiko) fish.

スパイダーロール

Spider Roll

soft shell crab tempura, tobiko (flying fish roe), lettuce

Soft shell crabs, while it may be hard to believe for the
uninitiated, are eaten whole, shells and all.
They are mild sweet, crispy, and unexpectedly delicious!

クリスマスロール

Christmas Roll

maguro (tuna), avocado, tobiko (flying fish roe)

The combination of rich red tuna and green avocado
give this popular roll its name.

アラスカロール
Alaska Roll

sake (salmon), avocado, cucumber

その他

Special Dishes and Unusual Sushi

This chapter introduces some special items from the world of sushi. Ingredients and presentations are quite different from nigiri and maki, so we encourage you to branch out. These delicacies number among rare opportunities and may introduce you to a new edible passion.

ちらし
[chi ra shi]

Scattered Sashimi Bowl

A medley of mostly uncooked ingredients
such as fish, shrimp, shellfish, vegetables, and egg,
served over a bed of rice.

いなり
[i na ri]

Bean Curd

vinegared rice stuffed inside
a pocket of abura-age (sweetened fried tofu)

hako-zushi maker

ばってら

[ba tte ra]

Boxed Mackerel

This hako-zushi is a specialty from the Kansai area (see page 11). The fish is topped with thin slices of vinegar-preserved kelp, *tera-kombu*, to prevent the fish from spoiling.

かに

[ka ni]

Boxed Crab

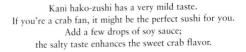

Kani hako-zushi has a very mild taste.
If you're a crab fan, it might be the perfect sushi for you.
Add a few drops of soy sauce;
the salty taste enhances the sweet crab flavor.

Unusual Sushi Toppings

Below are descriptions of some sushi toppings that are rarely found outside of Japan. If you encounter any of these, you should try them at least once.

ふぐ *Fugu*, or blowfish. The liver of the blowfish is poisonous to humans if the fish is not cut correctly; in Japan as well as in the United States, the sushi restaurants that serve fugu are required to have a special license. Today fugu is cultivated, so it's not as expensive as it used to be. Usually eaten as sashimi, the meat is sliced paper thin. The taste is very mild.

しゃこ *Shako*, or mantis shrimp. This crustacean is easy to differentiate from regular shrimp because the meat turns to a purplish color when cooked. The shako's roe are worth tasting.

Shako sushi

かにみそ *Kani miso*. This is the creamy green substance, called tomalley, found inside crabs. It may not look appetizing to some people, but for others this sushi topping is a favorite.

納豆 *Natto*. This form of fermented soybean seasoned with soy sauce and scallion has a very distinctive odor and taste. You will probably either love it or hate it; only a few of our American friends enjoy natto.

牛さし *Raw beef sashimi*. In Japanese cuisine, raw beef is commonly eaten, similar to the French tartare. Raw beef is usually served as sashimi, but in some areas of Japan it may be available as sushi.

Natto sushi

Kani Miso sushi

ACKNOWLEDGMENTS

All the sushi materials in this book were airmailed from Japan; thanks, Japan. Thank you to our hardworking photographer, Raeanne Giovanni-Inoue, for the beautiful sushi photographs and the warm cups of green tea. Thank you to our chef, Masayuki Nakano of Sushiden, for preparing gorgeous-looking sushi. Thank you to Sugao Yasumura, manager of Sushiden USA, for providing us with the sushi chef. Thank you to Minori's mom and dad for sending us the sushi props. Thank you to Kit's sister, Jenny Li, for financial support. A special thanks to the copy editor, Carrie Bradley, who did the bulk of the editorial work on this beautiful sushi book and the previous *Dim Sum* edition. And thank you to all the other people who contributed to this project. If we forgot to put your name here, we apologize. We still love you.

This book is designed by Minori Fukuda and Kit Shan Li, the parents of Work Eat Studio. Visit them at www.workeat.com.

BIOGRAPHIES

Minori Fukuda
is a graphic designer from Japan. She met Kit in the graduate program at the School of Visual Arts. She loves eating and cooking. She always thinks about dinner during her lunch.

Kit Shan Li
received her degree in design from the School of Visual Arts in New York City in 2003. She is not a professional cook, but she has loved food ever since she was born. She is adventurous when it comes to eating.

Raeanne Giovanni-Inoue
has been a New York–based photographer for more than twenty years. She specializes in photographing textiles, food, china, and glassware. She has traveled to Japan several times with her husband to visit family and learn about Japanese culture and food.

Masayuki Nakano
started training to be a sushi chef when he was eighteen years old. He began working as a sushi chef at the ANA Hotel in Tokyo, Japan, in 1982. He moved to New York to work at the Sushiden in 2003.